W9-DCU-609

WITHDRAWN FROM LIBRARY

CONFESSIONS OF AN ACTOR

© *Photo by Alfred Cheney Johnston*

John Barrymore and Daughter

CONFESSIONS OF AN ACTOR

BY

JOHN BARRYMORE

ILLUSTRATED

BENJAMIN BLOM, INC.

Reissued 1971 by Benjamin Blom, Inc., New York, N.Y. 10025
by arrangement with the copyright holder, The Bobbs-Merrill Company.

Reprinted from a copy supplied by courtesy of
the Wesleyan University Library

Library of Congress Catalog Card Number 70-84506

Printed in the United States of America

CONFESSIONS OF AN ACTOR

CONFESSIONS OF AN ACTOR

I

Cleveland's, on Wabash Avenue, Chicago, had been converted into a theater overnight. Before McKee Rankin and a man named Cleveland leased it for a season of repertoire, with Nance O'Neil as the star, the building had been a cyclorama of the Battle of Gettysburg. Needless to say, the structure was wholly unsuited for the new part it was to play, and the acoustics must have been reasonably peculiar. So far as I, a humble beginner, was concerned, neither the acoustics nor anything else mattered, for my performances on this battlefield were of Simon-pure badness.

When I played in Sudermann's Magda, I was given, as young Max, the brother of the heroine, a uniform which had been made for an actor of generous proportions. It was one of those supposedly form-fitting German frock-coat affairs with two rows of brass buttons down the front. It could not be taken in, and therefore the obvious thing was to build the wearer up for the uniform. Practically everything in the wardrobe that was not in actual use in the production was stuffed into that jacket, and still, as in the schoolboy's interior, there was ever room for more.

When I went on in the first act I had something of a chest, but when I took my normal position, which is like the letter S, the filling began to shift, and before many minutes I had as fine a stomach as any of the old-time New York policemen. I waited up all night in a warm saloon for the morning newspapers. There was only one notice. Amy Leslie said: "The part of Max was essayed by a young actor who calls himself Mr. John Barrymore. He walked about the stage as if he had been all dressed up and forgotten."

There is no more devastating tragedy than to be awfully bad at a job, to know that you are awfully bad and still not be able to do anything about it. McKee Rankin, who produced these plays, was a good stage manager, but he had too much to contend with and there never was any money in the theater. He had always to worry about bills. He could not waste time upon a fledgling actor, who wasn't any good anyway. The ordinary youngster who goes into the theater is stage-struck, and he has his ambition and illusion to carry him along and brace him up. I didn't even have the desire to succeed as a prop; I didn't want to be an actor. I was there merely because it was supposed that any member of a theater family ought to have something in him that would carry him through a crisis on the stage; at least he might be expected to possess a certain adaptability to the medium.

During these tragic and unhappy days I was living at a hotel that I was ashamed to mention when I chanced upon anyone who knew other members of the family. Early in my Chicago stay, at a sedate luncheon given by some friends of my sister, I had been asked where I was living. Quite casually I mentioned the name of my hotel. There was one of those awkward pauses that not even the politely noisy handling of knives and forks could quite cover. The hotel had been recommended to me by a philandering acquaintance who had had difficulties with other Chicago hostelries. After that I gave no address except Cleveland's Theater.

These same friends of Ethel were anxious to see me act and often threatened to gratify their curiosity. Knowing, as none knew better, just how bad I was, I kept putting them off and inventing reasons for the deferring of this treat. "Just wait," I would say, "till next week when we do Elizabeth. You must see me then. I shall

Albert Davis Collection

Ethel Barrymore as Nora in Ibsen's *The Doll's House*

Courtesy of Apeda

Mrs. Maurice Barrymore with her three children, Ethel, Lionel and Jack

be good in that, for I'll have a real part. I'll be no less a personage than Sir Francis Bacon."

But we never did the old play Elizabeth, in which Ristori made a very great hit many years before. A Denver creditor of McKee Rankin with little feeling for the drama, attached the scenery and properties because he had not been paid some trifling bill, and there never was money enough in the Chicago box office to send on to redeem this production. Ethel's friends tired of waiting, and one night, when I looked through a peep-hole in the curtain just before the play began, I saw them sitting like a jury in two center rows. I rushed back to my dressing room and applied more make-up, so that I might not be recognized. I had already worked for hours and I fancied that I looked like a character actor. I had used a little of everything in that make-up, but I was no more a character actor than a child would have been with a beard glued to its chin.

The bill for the evening was that good old stand-by of so many impecunious managers, Leah, the Forsaken. When I entered I was not recognized. My care as to make-up and my shingled blond wig baffled the people who knew me, but not for long. Then came my one line. As leader of the mob I had to say: "Throw her in the river." A howl went up from the front rows.

I was through, and in a few minutes I had the make-up off which had taken nearly five hours to put on. I dashed to the nearest Western Union office. Now it is generally known that in telegrams one may not transmit what are often the choicest bits of one's vocabulary, and the message which I had written out to my sister—"For Christ's sake send me fifty dollars"—was politely but none the less rejected. I was desperate. I knew that nothing but a most urgent message would be heeded. I could think of nothing strong enough that was good telegraphese. I explained to the trusting but somewhat doubting clerk that the message was not profanity at all, that I was an actor, that the manager of our company was a man called George W. Christ, and that it was on his behalf I wished the message sent. If it were not, the company would be stranded in Chicago. The message went—it also went with Ethel. I got the fifty dollars, and I left the theater and Chicago.

Another one of my beginnings in the theater was just after I had returned from two years at school in England. Ethel had made her great success in Clyde Fitch's play, Captain Jinks, and was playing a return engagement in Philadelphia. Francis Byrne, a member of her company, had left the cast unexpectedly, as his mother had died. There was no understudy and all the family thought that I ought to help Ethel out, though what I did to the performance that night was scarcely a help. I went to the theater as nonchalantly as if it were to a dinner that I had been summoned. I didn't know my lines, I didn't know where to stand or where to go. I seemed to have no sense of inherited responsibility. In the middle of my one good scene in the first act I forgot my lines and said to the naturally terrified and perspiring actor, who was on the stage with me, "Well, I've blown up! Where do we go from here?"

Ethel was scarcely able to speak one of her lines during the first act. When she would start one of her speeches, the player to whom it was addressed, seeing that she was helpless from laughter, would say, "Oh, don't you mean so and so?" And then he would give her speech. In this way the first act was finished. At the end of the second act there was usually a succession of curtain calls in which the star led the various members of the company out to the footlights. Instead I managed to be on the stage when the curtain went up and took a call all by myself. I thought that Ethel would pass out in the wings. Charles Frohman, who happened to be in the audience, told me that with a better memory he thought that I might make a comedian some day.

Of these early performances I have no play-bills and no scrapbooks. To my mind, at least, this is just one more evidence of my attitude toward the theater. I mean to be frank in these confessions, and I might as well state early in them that I didn't want to be an actor. I wanted to be a painter. I left the stage to study at art schools, and I only went back to the theater because there is hope—at least money—for the bad actor. The indifferent painter usually starves.

Ordinarily when a man writes of his work and his career, he is at the farther edge looking back. He weighs the disadvantages and the compensations, and almost invariably concludes that whatever his youthful ideas may have been, he really got into the right dimension of work, while to the youthful aspirant he would probably give Booth's counsel about going on the stage: "Don't do it." Still for himself his choice was inevitably right. I who write at what we may call the halfway point, am not quite so sure. But, on the other hand, if there is any value in these memories and confessions of mine, it may be because they are being set down on paper while I still have expectancy. So many memoirs, especially of the theater, are but faded memories and it is necessary not only to recall the incidents, but to set forth the reasons for recalling them as well.

I have written that I mean to be frank. I don't mind recording that I look upon myself as something of a second-story man. As a youth I was a good deal of a grafter. I appropriated other men's clothes and wore them—notably those of my uncle, John Drew, whose figure is *still* excellent! Once in England I overturned a punt and, having rescued my host's wife from the raging waters of the Thames and walked her ashore, I continued to live in that house all summer as a reward for my heroism, and borrowed my host's clothes because I had ruined mine in that foot of water of that hospitable stream.

As a boy I was, I think, a little more fruitful in untruth than my contemporaries. Also, I went in for theft. I stole my grandmother's jewels and hid them. While the detectives were in the house, I imagine I must have looked rather too casual for when my grandmother, Mrs. Drew, saw me, her one desire was to get rid of the detectives and talk to me with a well-worn slipper. Before this I had pilfered money from the other members of the family, in such small amounts that suspicion was not aroused. I carefully hoarded it till I had enough to buy a rosary for a symmetrical lady in Philadelphia, many years my senior, with whom I fancied myself in love. What strange inroads religion makes into the minds of the young!

Now, it is one thing to be frank and relate incidents which reflect no credit upon the teller, but for complete frankness, I feel I must set forth that I have a certain handicap that plays a most considerable part in my association with the theater. I am by nature and by the grace of God a very indolent person. Acting is a profession that requires infinite and intensive labor and patience, particularly in the creation of a character and the projection of a play. Because of my virtue of laziness, I have had to work doubly hard whenever I have accomplished anything at all in the theater. I have had to fight my own tendency to loaf as well as go through the very serious business of putting a play on. It isn't that I do not like rehearsal.

I enjoyed every minute of the long rehearsals in London, but then I usually have liked the rehearsals of any play. There is creation in the rehearsal period. Ever since I was a boy and wanted to be a painter I have had the urge to be a creative artist. In spite of the handicap of my laziness, that still holds. But when a production gets set and one must go to the theater six nights and two afternoons a week to repeat the same part, there is danger that after a certain time, even with the best intentions in the world, and with the most loyal and encouraging support of an audience, one may become stale. About this time one is reminded, as in the "big" love scene of the second act while breathing, with impassioned fervor, down the leading lady's neck, that fishing is perhaps a much better business. To play one part eight times a week is too much for any actor. If he is to have variety and freshness for his audiences, then he should have different material to work with. The only part that I have ever played that is always fresh to me is Hamlet. It is such a stark, blazing, glorious part, and he has such deathless things to say! And yet I know that I cannot play Hamlet eight times a week many weeks in succession.

CONFESSIONS OF AN ACTOR

People I meet so often ask me why I stop a play in what seems to them the middle of the run and while there is still a demand for seats at the box office. It is not easy to explain, but it is because I lack something that is a very valuable quality for an actor to possess. Not even the promise of great returns—and the business men of the theater tell me they would be good—can force me to cart myself, Hamlet and a lot of scenery around and play wherever they will let me.

The actor who is willing to repeat a part gains the greater facility by the repetition. And, besides, there are other advantages. He does not require so many vehicles, and he has the opportunity to build up a loyal following that may prove serviceable to him when, in the lean years that come to every actor, his personality is no longer a novelty. I am no trouper. To have that quality that makes for a good trouper is, as I say, of great value, but there are many valuable qualities that bring no particular pleasure to the possessor. Ambergris brings a great price by the ounce. It comes from the stomach of the diseased whale, but who would wish from choice to be the whale who makes this contribution? Not I. Perhaps I am selfish as well as lazy. I like that word "perhaps." It is easier to play a noble character on the stage and leave the nobility with the clothes and the make-up in the dressing room than to be a nice person off the stage.

The actor of to-day has an opportunity to get variety of work through acting in the films. In the beginning a great many persons of the theater and out of it looked upon the movies as an inferior art. It isn't. Pictures often go wrong just as stage plays do and are devoid of art. I was, myself, connected with what was probably the worst picture ever made. Not only did I play a part in this, but I had a great deal to do with the making of it. Come to think of it, it is quite a distinction that in all this great industry of the screen which has turned out so many bad pictures, I was largely responsible for about the worst picture I ever saw.

Not only may the actor gain variety of expression and work through appearing in the pictures, but he can earn enough money so that he may retire before he is too old. A man never knows when he is too old to play Romeo. The spirit is always willing, even if the flesh is all too visibly present. In the old days in the theater an aged Romeo was not infrequent. He may have looked perhaps like a corseted bloodhound, but he carried his lifted face proudly. He fancied that he could still play the part, and he did.

Though I came of an acting family and I have the heritage of an actor, I do not feel I am disloyal when I set forth my reasons for not caring too much for the theater as a medium in which to work. I don't believe when I was a boy I thought overmuch about what I should do

Mrs. John Drew as Mrs. Malaprop in Sheridan's *Rivals*

Miss Lane (the author's grandmother) at the age of eight as the five characters in *Twelve Precisely* from an old lithograph

when I grew up. In my grandmother's house there was often a discussion going on about acting, but it never seemed to mean anything to me or that I was part of it.

Of those days in Philadelphia I have few memories. There are a number of stories, wheezes we call them in the family, which are concerned with me, but I shall not tell them. They have been used by others of the family in their reminiscent articles and books and they have been told again and again by reminiscent writers outside the family. Particularly I shall not tell that story of my grandmother, Mrs. John Drew, Senior, and myself. The story I mean is the one in which I came home late for a meal and wanted to give a good excuse. I burst into the house and said: "Mummum, did you ever see a house that was painted all black?" Grandmother looked up, looked at me severely and said: "No, nor did you." I shall not tell that story.

CONFESSIONS OF AN ACTOR

At the age of nine, when I was at Notre Dame Convent in Philadelphia, I got into a fight with a schoolmate, and I threw a hard-boiled egg at him. I hit him right in the ear. It lodged there quite some time. As a punishment I was forced by the good Sister Vincent to look at a large book. It was Dante's Inferno, illustrated by Doré. From this I trace much of my later history. It opened up wide fields for me, things I had never dreamed of. It made such a lasting impression upon me that when I followed my own bent some years later and took up drawing, I tried to draw like Doré. And this incident, I think, accounts for much that is macabre in my character.

Later, when I was in Seton Hall School, in New Jersey, I was punished for some infraction of rules by one of my instructors, Father Marshall. I wrote an indignant letter to my grandmother, which ended with the sentence: "He struck me a blow which felled me to the ground."

My grandmother was horrified and sent my father instantly to find out if it was really true that I was being grossly ill-treated. Father was bored by the errand, but still he did not refuse a command from my grandmother. When he arrived at Seton Hall, however, he met Father Marshall first and got into a discussion with him about the Carlyle Harris case. Carlyle Harris was a student at The College of Physicians and Surgeons. He poisoned his young wife who was still a schoolgirl. He was arrested, tried and convicted of murder and was executed. The case was a great sensation at the time. With a talker like father it was soon time for his return train and he went away without seeing me. He merely left word with Father Marshall: "Tell the boy to look out and behave himself." My disappointment was very bitter, for I had let it be known that my father, who had been amateur heavyweight champion of England, was coming down to beat up the entire school. I had promised that there would be great ructions. It was an awful anticlimax.

I was alone with my grandmother the summer that she died. I can see her now as she sat there in her rocking-chair on the porch of an obscure hotel at Larchmont, New York. She had innumerable paper-backed books, and there was always one in her hands, but she seldom read. She sat gazing out across the Sound, but she was really gazing at old half-forgotten things, things that had once seemed important and which were now becoming confused in her mind.

Sometimes she would talk to me. She would break into the middle of a topic as though we had left it but a minute before. Mostly, she spoke of other times and other manners in the world of the theater. She was fond of me, fonder, I think I may say, than of any of her other grandchildren. At night when she went to bed I helped her to her room. I waited to be there to do this, though I wanted to go about nights and stay out until any hour. The day she died she reached over and patted me on the arm. To my mind, my grandmother typified everything that an actress should be.

What was the understanding, what was the rapport between this tired old woman of the theater and her wastrel grandson? Tired? Why shouldn't she have been? When she was eight years old she played five characters in a protean sketch called Twelve Precisely. There is a charming lithograph of her published in 1828 in these five characters. At eleven this same prodigy—she was Louisa Lane then—played Shakespere's King John. That was but the prelude to a busy, crowded life in which she was not only an actress, but for years manager of the Arch Street Theater in Philadelphia. Small wonder then that when she ceased to act she was tired.

After an absence of fourteen years, I went

back to the house in North Twelfth Street, in Philadelphia. It had seemed such a wonderful place to me, and the rooms had been so big; but now it was all drab and dreary. I do not know of what substance those conventional white Philadelphia steps are made, but they were being washed by a slatternly woman, and they did not seem to get much cleaner in the process. Those three steps that Ethel, Lionel and I had jumped up and down on in our countless trips in and out of that house. John Drew had crossed them to see his mother. Grandmother, with her stately dignity, had left from them to go to the theater. Jefferson, in his calls upon her, had walked there. It was perhaps on the second step that my mother stood one Sunday morning when she met my father as he was returning from an all-night party.

"Where are you going, Georgie?" he asked.

"I'm going to church. You can go to hell."

I went into the house and looked at the old

rooms where I had played, and of which I had such deathless memories. They were cramped and fusty. I saw the place on the top floor which was a cache for the things I stolē. I was really glad to leave and that I had a nicer place to go to—a theater where there was room to move about. In spite of the alien person washing the front steps, I did get back something of the personality of that wonderful old actress. Somehow I sensed the aura of Mrs. John Drew, even in that mean, shabby house. I felt something of her personality and austerity which she ever carried into the theater, where she was known as "the Duchess."

Of my mother I remember very little. I was very young when she died in California. When the news came to grandmother she was in New Jersey resting between seasons. She sent for me and told me of mother's death. She wanted to be alone with me then. Though my own knowledge of Georgie Drew Barrymore is slight, I am certain that she was a divine, gay, lovely person. Much has been written by actors and playwrights and literary people of Maurice Barrymore, my father—he was a great wit and his conversation kept people up willingly all night—but little has been said about my mother. A few years ago my wife, who was summing up her ideas of the Drew-Barrymore family, said: "What about your mother? She is the one who interests me most." The people who knew both my mother and my father remember mother best. Clever as my father was, he never pulled one of his famous lines upon her. He simply could not get away with it.

At the Lyceum Club at luncheon one day last winter in London, I sat next to Mrs. W. H. Kendall. She was kind enough to say some charming things about my Hamlet, which she had seen on the first night. She told me, however, that she was particularly interested to see me because I was the son of Georgie Drew

© *Photo by Sarony* © *Photo by Bradley and Rulofson*

Maurice Barrymore, the author's father

Mrs. Maurice Barrymore (Georgie Drew), the author's mother

An original drawing by the author

Barrymore, one of the most brilliant women she had ever known. Mrs. Kendall went on to tell me that she had made perfect havoc of father's witticisms, and he was supposed by everyone to be much the more witty.

In Nassau, where I was fishing with a genial old friend a few years ago, I met a charming lady who was living in the same house in Santa Barbara when mother died She told me of mother's death and that her last words were: "Oh, my poor kids, what will ever become of them?"

II

One doesn't have to go back so very far to remember when New York was still something of a village. There were fewer hotels and restaurants in those days, and though they may have been less comfortable, they were more friendly and they possessed more individuality. They stood for different things, and one patronized the restaurants and dining rooms to get certain dishes that one knew in advance one would find; just as one also knew that if he strolled into the bars that formerly dotted Broadway, he would encounter certain people at certain fixed hours.

There were fewer theaters, too, and when one of them had a first night it was sort of in the air. It seemed important somehow. Then the theatrical season began definitely with the opening of the Empire Theatre by my Uncle John Drew's company about Labor Day and ended usually about the first of May. Now the theatrical season practically never ends, and during most of the year there are four or five new plays a night staged in theaters that are as impersonal as the numbered streets from which they take their names, or else in theaters too new to have acquired the traditions that were associated with such names as Daly's, Wallack's, the Empire, the Madison Square, the old Lyceum, the Manhattan and the Fifth Avenue, where Mrs. Fiske's company put on the production of Becky Sharp, in which my father played Rawdon Crawley. When one walked along what was then known as the Rialto one met actors. And there was night life centered about Herald Square.

Even before the blight of Volsteadism, New York had evinced an impatience and a desire to change, to move up town and not to stay long when it got there. In this process of ever moving and rebuilding, the old theaters and the old haunts went and their places were taken, not by the same number of new structures but by many more than that. It was as if the gates had suddenly been opened to hordes of new people who demanded that they, too, must be fed and amused.

It is of a New York that is gone that I write, a New York that I first knew about the time of the Dewey Arch in Madison Square. I have a distinct memory of that arch that I suppose I may tell now. The statute of limitations must long since have put this deed of vandalism in that happy legal paradise where there is immunity from one's misdemeanors. After a dinner at Solari's restaurant, at which we changed the map of artistic Europe, three newspaper men, Carl Decker, Frank Butler, Rip Anthony, and I stole the sword from the hand of the figure of

Victory which surmounted the Dewey Arch. As I was the youngest, the most acrobatic and the least important all around, I played, not wholly from choice, the stellar part. I was assisted by boosts and shoves as far as the others could help me, and then I climbed aloft. I felt a good deal like Oliver Twist who used to be pushed through openings that Sykes and the others could not negotiate. We then paraded up Broadway with our dubious trophy, and the story of the exploit was told again and again in every barroom by the other three, all of whom were more fluent talkers, though less agile of limb, than I. It is difficult now to believe the absurdity that this huge thing of wood and plaster, divorced from its owner, the figure of Victory, should, when carried in mock triumph by the four of us, have proved an open sesame to places that, because of our poverty, were ordinarily barred to us. I do not know where we hid the sword when we went home.

At this time I was studying art. I had enrolled at the Art Students' League, but there I learned nothing. I went only once. I thought that my father, who had paid for the tuition, might be angry when he heard of this, but he merely said, "I can't understand how you happened to go once." I then went to a school run by George Bridgman. He took an especial interest in me, and helped me out of all proportion to what my demands upon his time should have been. I saw a good deal of him out of classes, and then he taught me more of life, observation and art than there was time to teach in the school.

I was interested, and I was working quite hard, and this seemed to impress the other members of the family. Ethel was talking about me one night to a great friend of hers, Cissie Loftus. "Isn't it a pity that Jack can't get started, that he can't get some recognition for his work?" Ethel said.

"What is his work?" asked Cissie in some surprise.

As a result of this conversation I was commissioned to do a poster for E. H. Sothern's production of Justin M'Carthy's François Villon play, If I Were King. Miss Loftus was the leading woman of the company, and she had talked to Daniel Frohman, Sothern's manager, about me. The poster was a good one and was used for many a year, and in after years when the play was revived it was used again. I have no embarrassment in mentioning how good this drawing was. Bridgman did most of it. I believe Mr. Frohman paid me five dollars for it.

Once at an exhibition of the Press Artists' League, a private affair run by a man who split with the artists if there was anything to split, I had the thrill of seeing a sticker with the magic word "Sold" pasted on a drawing of mine. It wasn't a cheerful subject: A hangman is walking along a road, carrying a stick which casts a shadow behind him, and this is so cast that it suggests a gallows. Above the road, floating in the air, are the faces of the men and women that the hangman has executed. When I had recovered from my shock that anyone should buy a drawing of mine—not that I didn't think it good, of course—I asked the name of the purchaser. Andrew Carnegie had thought The Hangman worth ten dollars. Of the purchase price I received five dollars, the maximum recognition of my talents.

During my days as an art student I saw a great deal of Rip Anthony and Frank Butler, two of the men who were associated with me in the theft of the plaster sword from the Dewey Arch. The former was familiar for some years to everyone along Broadway. Anthony was a tall, spare man with a pointed black beard. As I look back, his undeniable talent seems more wasted than that of almost anyone I have ever known. It made no money for him while he lived, and after his death he was remembered only by the people who had known his genial and buoyant self. He worked in wash, and he could do more to a piece of cardboard in half an hour than anyone I have ever seen use a brush. He had two salesmen, who, after the manner of that time, were described as bulldogs. They carried his work around telling an extremely pathetic story to any who would listen, that the artist was dying of tuberculosis; the irony was that Anthony did die of tuberculosis. When a picture was sold, Anthony got a third and each bulldog a third.

He lived in the old Aulic Hotel, which stood just opposite the side of the Herald Square Theater in Thirty-fifth Street. He managed to keep a room there, even though he seldom had money enough to eat. Again and again I saw him pull out a bureau drawer, use it for an easel and in an incredibly short time have a drawing done. In exchange for a night's lodging on the floor of his room, I often posed for him. I was all sorts of persons and figures. Once I was Custer's Last Stand, and at another time a Roman matron at the tomb of her son.

Anthony would go into the bar of the Aulic Hotel, or any place else along Broadway, without money enough to buy a drink, and would sit at a table waiting for some chance acquaintance to come in who might, in exchange for engaging conversation, purchase a highball. Several times when I joined him he would ask me in a loud voice to have dinner with him. We would sit at a table and bread and butter would be put before us. Anthony would immediately pocket the bread and some salt and pepper. We would seem to be waiting for someone before placing our order.

If no one turned up decently soon, Anthony would move on to his next prospecting ground. He would not do so, however, till he had left some such message as: "If Mr. Vanderbilt—or

Photo by Underwood & Underwood

An early photograph of John Barrymore

John Barrymore as Beau Brummel

Mr. Astor—comes in here asking for us, tell him we couldn't wait any longer and have gone on to Sherry's. They will understand." This obvious and transparent bluff was used again and again, but no one seemed to mind; no one even called it. The mornings after the nights that I would lodge with Anthony, there would be no breakfast except the pilfered roll of the night before. Anthony would put some hot water in a cup, salt and pepper it generously, and then call me to breakfast. "Get up," he would command, "we have bouillon this morning—bouillon, my boy."

In Thirty-fourth Street there was a boarding house run by a charming person called Minnie Hay, which was the gathering place for newspapermen. To-day one may meet an actor or a newspaperman any place or anywhere, but in the late nineties and for a while after, this was not true. The people in the professions used to be more clannish. There were fewer special writers and columnists then, and the news writer was not known through syndicates all over the country as he is now, but he was, I think, more widely known along Broadway and to his fellows than he is to-day. A story didn't have to be signed for the people at Minnie Hay's to know who wrote it.

Here one met everyone who wrote or drew for the papers. It was a friendly place, for in this clearing house for newspaper men no money was needed. Minnie was a philanthropist with no particular convictions in the matter. One just charged things. Somewhere in the Far West she had a husband, who sent her enough money to keep the place going. Saturday night this place became positively festive. Everyone did stunts. In those days no one danced except at a dance. Think of waltzing at a supper party in that period.

If one wanted to stand in well with the hostess as well as with the guests, one brought some delicacy to the Saturday night revels. A newspaper friend and I had been at three Saturday nights in succession without contributing anything except our presence. Another week, and we were still penniless. At a supper party during that week, Colonel John Jacob Astor had asked Ethel if she liked grapefruit, and she told him that she did. Grapefruit was something of a novelty then and had not as yet become part of the national breakfast. The next day a whole crate arrived at her house, which was just around the corner from the Garrick Theater, in Thirty-sixth Street.

This was a famous boarding house. Many people of the theater lived there, and at the time Maude Adams had an apartment there also. Ethel told me the incident of the grapefruit, and my friend and I went to call upon her when we knew that she was at the theater round the corner playing Captain Jinks. We borrowed the entire crate and took it to Minnie Hay's, where for one Saturday night we were the hit of the evening. Rip Anthony was a frequent visitor at Minnie Hay's, and it was there, I believe, that I first met Frank Butler.

Frank Butler was, I think, the most extraordinary man that I ever met. He was the son of a nephew of General Butler, of Civil War fame and his mother was Rose Etynge, at one time the leading woman of the Union Square Theater and a great favorite in New York. From the stories that were circulated about Frank Butler while he was alive, and that have lived in the conversation of a reminiscent turn of those who had the rare fortune to know this diverting individual, one might easily conclude that he was a far greater person than he actually was. I do not mean to imply that he was not an extremely able and facile writer, but he was what is usually described as a character, and in any age the designation of him would probably have been the same. Beau Brummel was such a character, as I found out when I played him on the screen—much more talked about and quoted than up and doing.

One afternoon, two years ago, during the run of Hamlet in New York, I went with two friends on an old-book hunt. This has some of the same lure for me as fishing, and it also requires patience. We were in an unfrequented bookshop on the West Side which specialized in foreign-language books, though there were a few sections of English books. On a shelf of verse I saw a slim book with the name "Butler," on the back. On the title page I found that it was written by Frank Butler, and that I had illustrated it. Till that day I had never owned a copy, and I had completely forgotten its existence. As I read it in the intermissions that night in my dressing room, many things that I had not thought of for nearly twenty years suddenly became fresh.

I seemed to see Butler—a happy Butler,

happy because he had his gold tooth. Somehow Frank Butler had managed to lose a front tooth, and in its place there was a detachable gold one. If his smile flashed the gold tooth he was to be trusted, he was affluent. If the gold tooth was not in sight it was pawned. It was the barometer of his fortunes. The limit of borrowing with this security was seventy cents. We often tried to get more but never did. It was his last asset and he never let it go without trying everything else to get money. Other historians of this same period have, when we have been swapping reminiscences, doubted this story of the gold tooth, but I vouch for its truth and can bring witnesses, if they are required.

One night when the gold tooth was not in his possession, I met Butler in Herald Square and he told me that of the usual seventy cents only fifteen was left. He had had no dinner, and he had no place to sleep. Both could not be done on that sum. I, too, had had nothing to eat, and

I had no money at all. I told Butler that I had a place to sleep, in fact, a studio in Fourteenth Street.

"If you feed me I'll lodge you."

He ruminated for a moment. "Done, by God!"

But he had that day written a story for the Morning Telegraph and his desire to read his own article was so great that part of the capital had to go for a copy of his paper. In those days the Telegraph was, I believe, the only morning paper that could be purchased the night before, and though it was a five-cent paper if one waited, ten cents was charged for the privilege of getting it before going to bed. Obviously our syndicate could not expend two-thirds of its capital on a paper, but Butler had to read his story and note what might have happened to it in the editing. He approached a newsboy and demanded a paper for five cents. The boy was at first unwilling to make such a sale, but he could not hold out long against the importance of the facts that Butler confessed about himself. Not only did he tell the boy that he worked for the paper, but he all but admitted that he owned the paper. At any rate, he got the Telegraph with the expenditure of but one nickel.

We then conferred as to the best way to spend the dime that remained. We agreed to repair to an all-night restaurant just around the corner from the Herald Building. The strategy was to be this: Butler, as the owner of the dime, was to go into the restaurant and order and pay for butter cakes, which were not only three for five, but were heavy and filling, and a cup of coffee. I was to wait outside till he had had time to eat one and one-half of the cakes and to drink one-half of the coffee. This I did and then entered. I looked about me a second and then found the table where he was sitting. I whispered something in his ear.

Butler suddenly pushed back his chair and

© *A Warner Brothers' Production*

John Barrymore as Beau Brummel

exclaimed dramatically: "My God, isn't that terrible!" He was to convey from his manner of exit that something had broken loose at his newspaper, presumably the near-by Herald, and that he was needed at once. He grabbed his hat, and, seeming to be choking from the insufficient food, he fled. I sat down to the unfinished meal, finished it, and then joined Butler round the corner.

We walked down to Fourteenth Street, and there I discovered that I had forgotten my key. Butler was not pleased with the prospect, but there was nothing for it but to sit down and wait until the furnace man arrived to receive the milkman. We wrapped pieces of the Morning Telegraph around us and sat on the brownstone stoop. At length we got in and climbed the weary steps to my hall room, which I had described as a studio. It was on the back and the one window faced north; to that extent it was a studio. I had never had any money to get any furniture, and there was nothing in the room except piles of books belonging to my father. These were strewn everywhere. Butler stood in the middle of the room, and with his pompous, outraged dignity, demanded, "Where do I sleep?"

I explained that he could have the middle of the floor or that vast space under the window, or he could take either side of the room. Then he knew he had been sold. Other floors might have been had for the asking, and he had paid in advance for the use of this one. He made the best of it and prepared to cover himself with books, as I did. We burrowed down into them as though they were snow. It was not a bad adventure for Butler, as he was able to turn the story of the night into copy the next day.

In that bare unfurnished room Butler dreamed that all the authors came to comfort us and offered us much of cheer and philosophy. "We were poor ourselves," they confessed, "until we attained recognition. You little know in what good company you find yourself and how much better bedfellows you have than if you had more money. It's not at all bad to be poor when you can have such distinguished company." This may seem far-fetched, but the story brought fifteen dollars. When he was paid, Butler gave me five dollars for my share in the evening. He had entirely forgiven me.

I had first heard of Butler from my brother, Lionel. He had played with him during a brief period when Butler, tired of writing, had desired to become an actor. He joined McKee Rankin's company, the same company with which I had played during my brief and unhappy engagement at Cleveland's converted cyclorama in Chicago. The company reached Minneapolis, and just as in the engagement at Cleveland's, times were very bad and no one had any money. Butler, Lionel and a man Lionel describes as the head of the Minneapolis underworld were sharing a room which they could not pay for; the underworld seems to have been at a low point there as well as the theater. In some way, Butler aroused the wrath of McKee Rankin, probably by his bad acting, and it must have been bad indeed to get a dismissal from a company when salaries were not being paid.

Now here comes a situation which is, I think, without parallel. Butler was let out on Saturday night, and on Monday he appeared in the front of the theater as the critic for the leading Minneapolis paper. When this was known behind the scenes consternation, envy and everything else were let loose, together with no little apprehension. Butler had gone to the editor of the paper Monday morning, and with his usual eloquence and persuasiveness had talked himself into a job. He admitted to knowing everyone in the East. One of his modest assertions was that he was a friend and protégé of Charles A. Dana, the owner of the New York Sun.

Now it happened that the regular dramatic critic wanted to get up in Canada on his vacation. It was the end of the season, and the Rankin company had taken the theater to play repertoire as long as they could compete with the parks and the open spaces. It was scarcely worth while for the critic to delay his vacation, and Butler got the job. No dismissed actor ever had a chance like this, and Butler made the most of it. No one who knew him doubted but that he would.

The company, never too thoroughly rehearsed, had little confidence that Monday night. The play was an adaptation from the French, and both McKee Rankin and Nance O'Neil played titles. The critic lost no time in his review in pointing out to the good people of Minneapolis that not only were the two leading actors unfamiliar with persons of rank, but that there was nothing Gallic about them or their performances. His invective against Rankin was as skilful as it was unfair. No ordinary critic could have put this thing into type in a way that would have hurt so much.

Then Butler went on to point out that even with the example of all this bad acting before him he could not see how any actor could play as relatively unimportant a part as that of the servant so atrociously that it seemed almost important. This was Lionel, with whom he was sharing a room, for which Butler ultimately paid, as there were no salaries for the actors during this engagement. Fortuitously for him, Butler lasted as critic as long as the Rankin company stayed in Minneapolis, and he made more than enough money to get back to New York.

In addition to his work as dramatic critic, he did signed Sunday articles about Minneapolis which were far from flattering to the town. He would begin these articles—I remember one particularly which began, "Five o'clock, the hour of absinth in Paris." Then he went on to describe life at that time of day in Paris. Then he wrote of what five o'clock meant in New York—less romantic, but still interesting; and thus, by easy stages, and filling a column and a half of space, he arrived at Minneapolis at five o'clock, where nothing happened at all. Then he would launch into one of his invective attacks upon the street railway company, the gas company and politics in general in the town, about which he knew nothing.

Butler's writing, particularly of invective, always seemed to me to be extraordinarily good. He had style which, alongside of some of the slangy, present-day newspaper writing, was almost Johnsonian. And he could write with charm and whimsicality, as he did in the story of the books. Just as in the case of Rip Anthony, a great deal of natural ability and bitterly acquired experience went to waste. I lost track of Butler for a while, and then I heard of his death. This must have been hastened by the life that he had led, the uncertainty of food and lodging, the lack of even the most ordinary comforts and a preying, almost childish, loneliness.

During these early vagabond days I continued my study of art with Bridgman as long as I could, and now and then I sold a drawing. I could almost always get a dollar by doing a drawing for the advertising of a certain clothing firm, and once for twenty minutes I was on the staff of the New York Telegraph. I went there one morning and asked if there was a vacancy in the art department, and was told that there was. The editor gave me, without seeing me, the assignment to copy in line Gainsborough's portrait of the Duchess of Devonshire. It took me just twenty minutes to make the copy, and then word was sent out that it wouldn't do, and I was fired.

While I was looking for a chance to draw for some paper I went into a peculiar business for one who wished to be an artist. The product we were to sell was a lotion to be used after shaving, and it was called after its discoverer, Schaeferine. For this important concern I was, oddly enough, the testimonial getter. The job was given to me because I was the nephew of John Drew, and in our advertising there appeared this statement: "John Drew uses and indorses Schaeferine." For this I once more got five dollars, and I was told that for every testimonial I could get there would be another five.

When our preparation was put upon the market it was intended that it should be used only by men, but because there was a prospect that I might be able to get an indorsement from my sister, it was changed to a general face lotion. Ethel was away and I telegraphed her urgently. For many anxious days no reply was received in the office of the Schaeferine Company, and then this message came: "Dear Sirs: I received your—I can't remember the damned thing's name—but I think it's the best table water I ever drank."

While I was waiting for this reply I approached other celebrities. Nat Goodwin gave the company a serious testimonial and then sent me one personally: "I have used your Schaeferine—my lawyer will see you in the morning." The Schaeferine Company did not last long, because the product cost fifty cents to make and thirty cents a bottle to sell. At this rate there could be no profit. When the company went out of existence I was once more confronted with "Where do we go from here?"

After an interval, I succeeded in getting into the art department of the New York Evening Journal, where I worked for eighteen months. During this time I did a variety of conventional newspaper work, but usually my drawings illustrated something on the editorial page written by Arthur Brisbane. I had been tremendously impressed as a child by the drawings of

Doré and my work now showed this influence. My drawings were of a symbolic, allegorical character and steeped in gloom.

I illustrated some of the verses of Ella Wheeler Wilcox and she protested to Arthur Brisbane: "Don't let that pessimistic old swine, Barrymore, illustrate anything more of mine." The combination was an extraordinary one, for she was a poetess of optimism. Arthur Brisbane sent me up to the Hoffman House to see her.

My timid knock was answered by the poetess herself, who was wearing a flowing light-blue velvet dressing gown. "I am Barrymore," I said.

"Didn't your father have courage enough to come up here himself?" she asked.

I then explained that I was the artist who had offended her, and we had a long talk in which I confessed some of my shortcomings. My study of anatomy had not progressed so far as the human feet, and there was always long grass hiding feet in my drawings. When I left, Mrs. Wilcox, who was a grand soul, called up Brisbane and told him that she didn't want anyone else to illustrate her verses.

Though my work was usually on the editorial page and did not always reflect the immediate news of the day, it was a news item that caused a good deal of a stir that led to my being fired from the Evening Journal. Paul Leicester Ford, the novelist who wrote Janice Meredith, was shot and killed by his brother, Malcolm. I was to make a drawing of this, but on the day of the happening, I got to the office late—as I so often did—and my drawing could not be reproduced as it ordinarily was in half half-tone. It had to be reproduced in the quickest way, which was an ordinary half-tone reproduction, and it came out badly. There was no time to do anything about it and the botched drawing was reproduced. Mr. Brisbane had written a very powerful article on the subject of this crime, in the middle of which he wrote: "The picture on this page illustrates" so-and-so. It was so badly done, however, that it showed only that the artist had been out late the night before.

Mr. Brisbane sent for me to come to his office. He had the paper stretched before him, open at the offending page. "Barrymore," he asked, "you were an actor, weren't you, before you came here?"

I admitted to having been on the stage, though not importantly.

"Well," he continued, "don't you think you could ——"

I didn't know whether I could or not, but I had to; so I did.

III

On a night in April, 1906, I was sitting in a box in the Grand Opera House, Mission Street, San Francisco, hearing a performance of Carmen sung by Caruso, Madame Fremstad and others of the Metropolitan Opera Company of New York. I had been playing with Willie Collier's company in Richard Harding Davis' play, The Dictator, and we had closed our season in San Francisco the Saturday before. We were to sail for Australia the next day. Carmen, the first opera of what was intended to be only a short season and turned out to be but an engagement for one night, drew a marvelous and appreciative audience; all of San Francisco and his wife was there. Most people perhaps have forgotten that Fremstad sang Carmen. It was not one of her great rôles, like her Isolde, but it was a competent performance, and because Fremstad, a blonde, did not wear a dark wig, there had been a good deal of advance advertising. But within a few hours, however, not even a blonde Carmen was a topic for talk. Man's affairs suddenly became very unimportant.

After the opera I went to a supper party and between three and four I walked home with a friend to his house. We talked a while, and then he insisted that I must look at some pieces of old Chinese glass that he had just received. Upon this collection my friend lavished all of his leisure and a great deal of money. It got so late that I decided to sleep where I was and not go back to the St. Francis Hotel. I had only been in bed a few minutes when the earthquake—the first great shock—occurred. It all but threw me out of bed. I put on my evening clothes again and went out into the hall, where I found the valet trying to wake his master, without success. An earthquake or the fact that his house was all askew did not disturb him, but when I went into his room and shouted at him "Come and see what has happened to the Ming Dynasty," he jumped out of bed, for he was a true collector. The collection in which he had taken so much pride was shaken into little more than a mere powder of glass.

There was nothing for us to do there, so we walked toward town. Everywhere whole sides of houses were gone. The effect was as if someone had lined the streets with gigantic dolls' houses of the sort that have no fronts. People were hurriedly dressing and at the same time trying to gather and throw out what seemed most valuable to them. More prudent persons, who couldn't too readily shake off the habits of shyness nor too quickly forget their decorum, were putting up sheets to shield themselves from the passers-by.

I was going into the St. Francis Hotel when

John Barrymore as Beau Brummel

John Barrymore as Richard III

I heard Willie Collier call to me, "Go West, young man, and blow up with the country." He was sitting just opposite the hotel in Union Square, wearing bedroom slippers and a flowered dressing gown.

The square, into which so many oddly dressed persons and their belongings had been hastily thrown, presented a strange, almost uncanny appearance. Ordinarily this open space is dominated by the column which Robert Aiken designed to commemorate Dewey's victory. This had shifted to a slight angle, so slight that it was found in the rebuilding of San Francisco that by shaving off the column and making it cylindrical instead of fluted, it would be true and stand straight. But the figure on top had turned completely round on its axis, and presented the most rakish appearance. Just near by, sitting calmly on one of her trunks, and surrounded by others, and with an excitable French maid hovering about and contributing largely to the general excitement, was a lady I had never seen before. It was cold that morning in Union Square, between five and six.

"Aren't you cold?" I asked her. "Can't I get you something?"

Though lightly clad, she was charmingly unperturbed. I was much the best-dressed person on the Square, and she seemed greatly amused by my solicitude. "Certainly," she said, "if it isn't too much trouble."

I walked up Post Street to the Bohemian Club and while there fortified myself. I then proceeded back to Union Square, carrying a glass of brandy in my hand. As I remember, I spilled most of it. I learned afterward that the lady whose poise was so perfect in these strange surroundings and who was so grateful for my attention was Madame Alda, of the Metropolitan Opera Company.

If ever people needed stimulants they needed them that morning, and the bar in the St.

Francis Hotel was soon opened to an excited group of people, all of whom talked at once and no two of whom agreed as to what they had seen; in fact, I find that no one believes anyone else's stories of what he saw during those few days. People have often doubted mine, particularly that I went to help a friend bury a trunk containing some of his choicest possessions in an empty lot, and that afterward neither he nor I could remember where these things were buried.

I walked about the streets and ran into many people I knew. I saw Caruso with his trunks on a van; and in front of the Palace Hotel I found Diamond Jim Brady, that inveterate first nighter of New York. He was amused to see me in evening dress, and when he went back East he and many others circulated this story about my dressing for an earthquake; in fact, a great deal of my reputation for eccentricity had, I think, its origin in this incident. Until I talked to Brady it had not occurred to me that I was oddly dressed for the occasion. I don't know, though, what one should wear at an earthquake.

As I was getting very sleepy I went back to the St. Francis and went to the desk to get my key. The clerk started to talk to me and to tell me that there was a split in the front of the hotel. I asked him if it was safe to go up to my room.

"Perfectly," he said, with the trained assurance of a Californian. "There isn't the slightest chance in the world of it ever happening again."

Just then the second version, which was a little before eight o'clock, shook the whole place angrily, and the clerk jumped across the desk and, with what seemed to me like one motion, was out in Union Square. It was not so much a jump as it was a dive. It reminded me greatly of the old extravaganza, Superba, in which the Hanlon Brothers, of pleasing memory, used to make the most surprising entrances and diving exits from the stage. I went back of the desk, took my own key out of the box and walked upstairs to my room and went to bed. I slept till late afternoon, when I was awakened by the general excitement in front of the hotel and the smell of things burning in the distance. My trunks had been made ready for Australia the day before, and had gone to the baggage room or somewhere else on their way. I never recovered them.

In taking some clothes out of a bag that was partly packed, I discovered a gun which had been given to me by Chief of Police Delaney of Denver. I met him while I was playing with my sister in a play called Sunday. I acted the part of a young man who kills the villain in the first act. With my gun play I had one line: "He had to die." This always got an unintended laugh. Chief Delaney told me that he intended seeing the play, and I promised him that I'd use the gun he had given me. I pulled it out and though it was a good murderous weapon, with which, before it became police property, a Chinaman had killed his wife, it failed to fire the blank cartridge. As ever in an emergency like this, the stage manager fired a gun backstage. As I said my line, "He had to die," the smoke of the other gun floated on to the scene from the wings and was quite visible. Never before had the audience had such a good laugh over this, though the line was always a cue for a magnificent one. Somehow one night there was no laughter at all. The line was taken seriously. I had become better in the reading of it, and after that there was never any trouble again. I think it was in San Francisco that this unaccountable change took place.

And this reminds one that we are in the midst of an earthquake, and that a fire is spreading rapidly through a whole city. I put Chief Delaney's gun in my pocket and walked up to the house of some friends on Van Ness Avenue. The family were making a hurried preparation to leave for Burlingame, and I tried to help them. Rumor had spread that both sides of Van Ness Avenue were to be blown up with dynamite to make a wide ditch that might stop the fire. The small-scale dynamiting which had been done up to this time had accelerated rather than stopped the spread of the fire. As I walked through that house, trying to find valuables which were to be packed, I saw that in an upper room the dresses that the two daughters of the house were to wear at a ball at the Presidio that night had been laid out the night before.

From this same upper room, which had no front wall, I saw Walter Hobart, a great friend of mine, go to a house which he owned across the street. I ran down and across to him. He had heard, too, that all of Van Ness Avenue was to be blown up, and he had come to get two great treasures—a painting by Rochegrosse of an Assyrian king shooting lions, and the other a bust of himself as a young boy which had been done by Falguière. He had not been in this house for fifteen years. It was the old family residence, and he had no key. In the earthquake the house had not been sufficiently damaged for us to enter without breaking a window.

Just as we were picking out the glass from the frame a man dashed around the corner with the biggest-looking gun I have ever seen, though I am assured that all guns aimed at one assume gigantic proportions. Fortunately, the man behind the gun asked questions before he shot. It took a great deal of persuasion, however, to convince him that two unshaven men, who had just smashed a window, were not doing it for the purpose of loot. Also Hobart's story that he owned the house and had not been in it for fifteen years was far from convincing. Finally, we did get in, and secured the bust and painting which we cut from the frame, wrapping it around the bust.

I went back to my friends across the way and with them I drove to Burlingame. Here we stayed in an untenanted house, owned by some people we knew, for six days. I hoped that by that time the company was well on its way to Australia. I never had any desire to go on that trip anyway, and now I felt that I had seen something of the wonders of Nature during the earthquake. After playing lost for six days, it occurred to me that I ought to get word to my family and to the Frohman office, by whom I was employed. I borrowed a bicycle and started for San Francisco. I was given a lift part of the way, but I entered the destroyed city on my bicycle. I had been quite familiar with the town, but all the landmarks were gone, and it was the strangest effect, riding through those streets which were nothing but ruins, and it was with the greatest difficulty that I found the Oakland Ferry. My friend, Walter Hobart, had given me his police badge, with which he assured me I would have no trouble in getting to Oakland, but some soldiers from the Presidio, seeing the badge which I displayed conspicuously, stopped me and put me to work bossing a gang of men who were sorting out and piling up débris. I knew so little about work myself that it was difficult for me to become a good executive. After about eight hours of make-believe I was allowed to proceed to Oakland.

The first person I met as I got off the boat was Ashton Stevens, the dramatic critic. Thinking to give me good news, he said: "You're in time to get your boat after all. Word was sent East, 'Everybody found except Barrymore.' The company is going to sail from Vancouver in three days." I then learned that the boat on which we were to have sailed for Australia had been commandeered by the owner of the line, in order to get his wife, who was ill, out of the city. I wanted to turn back and be lost a little while longer, and I would have done so if I had not just then encountered Jack Dean, another member of the Collier company. There was nothing for it but to go to Australia.

In Vancouver I found that I had ten dollars and no clothes, except the ones I had on, and these had suffered greatly in the days following the earthquake and were far from presentable. For five dollars I bought a blue serge suit which did not take kindly to the damp air, and when we had been at sea a few days it shrunk so that I was the butt of the other members of the company whenever I appeared.

Having purchased this blue serge, I went to a hotel and wrote a long letter to my sister. I wanted to make it a good one and worth at least a hundred dollars, so I described in great detail what I had seen in those harrowing days and what I had myself been through. I confessed to having seen people shot in the street, spiked on bayonets and other horrors so great that the imagination was almost blunt from contemplating them. I wrote that I had been thrown out of bed by the earthquake and almost miraculously escaped injury from falling bricks and plaster, and then, with much pathos and resignation, I described the terrible scene at the Oakland ferry where, weak from exhaustion and privation I had been cruelly put to work sorting stones by the soldiers.

Ethel was reading this letter sympathetically to our uncle, John Drew, and during one of the best bits he was so strangely quiet that she stopped and asked: "What's the matter, Uncle Jack? Don't you believe it?"

"I believe every word of it," he answered. "It took a convulsion of Nature to make him get up and the United States Army to make him go to work."

In Australia we played both The Dictator and Augustus Thomas' play, On the Quiet. We opened in the former, and at the end of the second act there was a most friendly demonstration. Flowers were handed over the footlights for the women of the company and someone had sent Collier a puppy about a week old. In the

© *A Warner Brothers' Production*

John Barrymore and Dolores Costello in *The Sea Beast* (Moby Dick)

John Barrymore as Capt. Ahab in *The Sea Beast* (*Moby Dick*)

next act when the scene was reached in which the Central American general, an all-round bad man, tells the character played by Collier that he is going to kill all the Americans, and ends with the defiant words, "What can you do about it?" Collier was supposed to reply patriotically, "I'll appeal to the American Government." But he could not miss a chance to put in a line of his own; he was quite willing to gag or interpolate on an opening night on a new continent, vital though that night might be to the success of the expedition. He said, instead of the customary line, "Why, I'll sick my dog on you." It naturally went with a yell.

In Australia we were asked about a great deal, and one day we attended a ghastly luncheon. It was one of those affairs that are sometimes given by a college professor or a clergyman who desires to prove that he is broad-minded and therefore he entertains a theatrical company. It was a clergyman this time, I believe. We had gone through all the usual questions that are asked actors by people unfamiliar with the stage: "Do you make up your own face?" "Do you live the part you play?" "Do you enjoy acting every night?" We parried these as well as we might without seeming to be too rude. Now there was in the company a young man who was very shy, and he had said nothing at all. Finally, our host noticed this, and wishing to put him at ease, asked, "Do you have absolute control over your face?" This shy young man, who was one of those one-remark young men, answered quickly: "My God, no! If I had, it wouldn't look a bit like this." Then he subsided into his silence, in which he was left undisturbed.

Melbourne is not a city, at least it was not during our engagement, where the actor finds places to go to supper and sit up and talk. The proprietor of a delicatessen store gave us the use of a room over his shop. There was only one gas jet, and night after night we sat in the dusty dinginess, because literally there was no other place to go. The company had played together for three years. We had been on a long sea voyage together, we had listened to and doubted one another's stories of the earthquake, and not one of us had anything in his past or future left to talk about.

One night when we were leaving the theater we saw in the foggy distance a figure that arrested our jaded attention. Even in the murk of Melbourne, we could see that he was prodigiously drunk and a resplendent figure in a high hat, a thrown-back Inverness coat and a shirt front like the advertisement of the Hoffman House cigars. As we neared him he flung out his arm, after the manner of the father of Meredith's Harry Richmond, and said in a voice of Falstaffian sonority: "Birds of the night, whither away?" He was full of language like that.

He was far too good for us to lose, bored as we were with one another, and we haled this picked-up and brushed-up acquisition in triumph to our mortuary supper table. But we no sooner sat down than our newly acquired friend went sound asleep. Collier was talking about the business that we had done—we had not been a gigantic success—and he was consoling himself and us with the fact that other American companies had not been too successful in Australia. He began talking about the failure of Nat Goodwin in Melbourne and Sydney.

Our sleeping friend, at the mention of the name Goodwin, woke up and said: "Goodwin! Goodwin? Um-m—Nat Goodwin was once preeminent in sententious comedy, but now—hic—if you will permit me to say so—he is—hic—*erstwhile.*" He was a one-remark man, too, and he said nothing else the rest of the night.

On our way back from Australia, Collier and

I allowed our beards to grow, and we had much amusement anticipating that we would go into the Frohman offices in New York and say, "This is what Australia has done to us." But upon arriving at Vancouver, we found that we should have to shave, for the company was booked to play all the way back East before disbanding. It was a great education to be with a man like Willie Collier, who was never at a loss for a moment on the stage. He was marvelously quick to sense if anything was going wrong, and he was equally quick to make things go wrong to divert the other actors.

Early in his career Collier had played with an old minstrel comedian, Charles Reed, who had a great reputation for gagging and interpolating. Collier learned everything that Reed knew, and then developed the art himself. This sort of thing, which does not make for the serenity of playwrights, has practically passed out of the theater. At the dress rehearsal of The

Dictator, Collier had Richard Harding Davis in a state of positive panic. Hardly any of the play was written by Davis that night.

I played in this piece not only all over this country and in Australia, but in London as well, where A. B. Walkley, writing in The Times, gave me faint praise, but did not mention my name. He referred to me as—"a gentleman who appears as a wireless telegraph operator and offers a choice anthology of American slang."

This long association was very pleasant, extraordinarily instructive, and I think only twice did I annoy Collier. Once during the New York run I went to bed in the late afternoon leaving a call for seven o'clock. It was naturally thought that I meant seven in the morning, and it was nine o'clock when I woke up. I rushed to the theater and found that the understudy, Wallace McCutcheon, had played my part during the first act. Collier very wisely refused to let me go on for the rest of the play, as the understudy had already appeared before the audience. Having nothing else to do, I went to the front of the theater and sat in one of the boxes, with some rather swell friends of Ethel. No one in the theater that night applauded so much or so loudly as I did. I should have been fired, but somehow I wasn't.

In Chicago, Collier delivered an ultimatum, and that was that I purchase a new pair of white duck trousers. The only pair I had were covered with bolarmenia and other make-up and they were quite disgraceful. Collier insisted that I buy a new pair. He told the men of the company that he didn't care whether I borrowed from them, but if there was a spot on the borrowed trousers, the owner, as well as myself, would be fired. It was too great a risk and no one would let me borrow, so I was forced to go to Marshall Field's to buy a pair of white duck trousers, but as it was February and people didn't go to Florida so feverishly in those days, their stock was not easily accessible. After a long delay the only pair I could wear at all was discovered, and these were much too small for me. When I came out on the stage that night Collier at once noticed that I had to move about with care. I appeared literally molded or poured into the trousers. It was a chance after his own heart. "Young man," he said to me, "you work too hard." He placed a chair for me. "Do sit down." It was some minutes before he allowed the play to continue, and I had to stand there, not daring to move. The next night the dirty trousers appeared again, and they were never mentioned.

At another time during the Chicago run when I was in the good graces of the star, I found when I came on the stage that, entirely to divert me, Collier had made himself up to look like my uncle, John Drew. On still another occasion, when he thought he had played too long in a certain town, he went to great trouble to make up Thomas Meighan, who played the United States Marine in the last two minutes of the play, as an old man with a long gray beard.

My next job was in a play called Half a Husband, in which Emily Stevens was the leading woman. At the dress rehearsal in New York there were very long intermissions and a great many people came in. We had supper brought in, drank a good deal of champagne and discussed the play amicably. No one knew just how long the piece was. As I remember, we opened in some little town which was reached by motor from Syracuse. Here, to the consternation of the management, it was found that even with the utmost generosity on the part of the orchestra—they played everything they knew and one man, heavily encored, did a xylophone solo; he was the only hit of the evening—even with all this help, the play ran less than an hour and a half and the final curtain came down at nine-thirty.

Arnold Daly, who produced the play, had

written in a love scene for me. I had never played one, and I didn't know how to. I don't remember the story of the play, but in any event I was too late for my wedding, and the bride refused to marry me. I entered and saw her in the arms of another man. I said, "God bless you!" and that was the end. Earlier in the play there was a scene in which a table in the center of the stage figured. It was filled with supposed wedding presents—awful horrors from the property room of this small-town theater. I had some line about these gilt caskets and fruit dishes, but when I saw them for the first time, remembering my long training with Collier, if not my line, I said: "Ah, I see father has been playing pool again." I imagined the audience knew the "props" from other plays, and it was the only thing I said that night that got over.

I was broke once more and in Atlantic City. A certain set of lapis lazuli cuff-buttons, which I rather liked, had already gone, and my hotel bill

John Barrymore as Hamlet

John Barrymore in *The Stubborn Cinderella*

was getting worse and more unpayable. I was in a situation like this in London once, years ago. I had a cab and no money to pay for it. Everywhere I drove I was turned down, and every time I approached a new prospect I had to ask for more money than I had just been refused, as the cab bill was mounting. When I finally found a complacent person to lend me some money, the cab bill was four pounds. At Atlantic City that night I was dining alone, eating some shrimp bisque—I have never eaten it since—when Mort Singer, the theatrical manager, came up and began talking to me. He told me that he was putting on a new musical piece called A Stubborn Cinderella, at a new theater in Chicago. "Would you like a part in it?" he asked.

"Oh, I don't know; I've got something in mind that I'm considering." All I was considering was what the hotel might do to me and who was going to pay for the shrimp bisque.

"How would a hundred and fifty dollars a week do?" asked Singer.

Up to this time my salary had not been over fifty dollars a week, and I was so staggered I couldn't answer.

Singer looked at my blank countenance, and thinking that I was hesitating because he had not offered enough, said: "Well, then, make it a hundred and seventy-five. If you want some money now, here is a hundred dollars."

By that time I had found my voice, and I accepted the offer.

The plaster was scarcely dry in the Princess Theater when A Stubborn Cinderella opened, and the production seemed to the company destined to quick failure. After the first night, at which the audience had not been particularly responsive, Walter Hackett, the playwright, Lou Houseman and I went to a café known as The Bucket of Blood, where we talked all night about things and changes that might be done to save the piece from utter failure, though we honestly thought there was little chance. Our discussion was interrupted by the arrival of the late edition of the morning papers. The critics pronounced A Stubborn Cinderella the best show that had been in Chicago for years. It ran for two years. It never was a success in New York. I did a song and dance in it.

Then I played in a number of plays and in three of Barrie's with my sister—Alice-Sit-by-the-Fire, Pantaloon and A Slice of Life, but I never had a real chance until I was cast for the part of young Nat Duncan in Winchell Smith's play, The Fortune Hunter. It didn't go very well at rehearsals, and after the first night in New Haven the management was in doubt about letting me go into New York. Finally—perhaps they had no other juvenile—they let me try it, and I was a success—my first real hit in the theater. One's first success? How did it happen? Whoever stops to think of such things?

In other arts people strip their souls naked in mean attics year after year, but in the theater one may win recognition overnight. But then, in the theater one is never safe. At any minute one may show himself up. It is easier to get on and up in the theater than to stay put.

But while I was pondering over this brand-new state of things for me—being a hit in the theater—there came to me a disturbing, somewhat saddening thought. From now on I had a career, it seemed, which I could no longer kick in the slats. It was good-by to the irresponsibilities of youth. I had happened to be fairly good at them.

John Barrymore in *The Fortune Hunter*

John Barrymore in Galsworthy's *Justice*

IV

In a melodrama of New York's underworld, called Kick-in, I had my first opportunity to do serious work in the theater. In its original form Kick-in had been a one-act play which the author, Willard Mack, used to play on vaudeville circuits. The one serious scene of the expanded version was practically the whole of the one-act play. While I was playing the part of Chick Hughes in Kick-in, Edward Sheldon, the author of Romance and Salvation Nell, came to the theater to see me. I had first met him when I was playing the young hero in a play that he had written, The Princess Zim Zim. This play, which was tried out in Albany, moved on to Boston, but never made an attack upon New York, had an excellent first act in which a supposedly swell young man on a spree goes to Coney Island and while he is bathing in the early hours of the morning, his evening clothes are stolen. He is forced to take refuge in a dime museum where they give him some clothes. Here he stays on as the piano player as he becomes interested in the snake charmer.

During the rehearsals and the short run of Zim Zim, I saw a good deal of Sheldon and he became interested in my work. No one since I have been a serious actor has been more helpful to me than Edward Sheldon; in fact I am not sure that he didn't make me a serious actor. That day he came to my dressing room during the run of Kick-in, he said: "If I were you I should play a part without a bit of comedy in it. As long as you do both comedy and straight work in one play, they will always think you a comedian."

"I suppose that I might try it," I said. "I could paste down my mustache."

My first thought was not of what I might do in the serious part, but that a great many serious parts might require me to make the sacrifice of my mustache. To me, then, this seemed a thing not to be too lightly parted from. Pasting down was an old expedient of the theater and in the palmy days many vain actors refused, regardless of the period they were supposed to represent, to sacrifice their facial adornment. It is an old story of the theater that Edwin Forrest, whether playing in a contemporary play or one of the Roman period, always wore the side and the little chin whiskers. As Spartacus he looked like a venerable rubber in a Turkish bath.

Sheldon, however, did not dismiss the matter so readily or so lightly as I did. He persisted. When he found that Galsworthy's play, Justice, was to be put on, he arranged with the producers that I play the leading part of the defaulting clerk. I went at it with no little trepidation. The play was produced for the first time in New

Haven, Connecticut, which had also been the scene of my first comedy hit in The Fortune Hunter. On the opening night when I pounded with frenzy upon my cell door in the prison, I broke right through the wood grating, which was painted black as an understudy for iron. Few persons outside of the theater have any comprehension of how strong an actor is on the first night. He is worked up to such an intensity through fear, I suppose, that he can do almost anything of the Samson or Sandow character. Actually, I believe that a midget playing a tragic part, if he was wrought up to the proper pitch of panic, could, on a first night, lift a grand piano.

A. Toxin Worm, who was for many years associated with the business end of the theater, and was, just before his death, press agent for the Shuberts, in commenting upon the first night of Justice, which he went up to New Haven to see, said: "I don't think very much of it.

It's dull, and I suppose it's deep; there's only one good scene and that's the one where Barrymore busts the prison door and makes his escape." Thereafter, the door was sufficiently reenforced with metal so that no one in the audience might think that I made my escape and thus miss the point of the play.

When we came into New York for a few rehearsals before opening, I found that in front of the Harris Theater in Forty-second Street and in the lobby, there were bills and posters featuring my name. I went round with strips of paper and pasted out this display. For a short time I was given credit for modesty, but it was not that. It was shrewdness, I think, for I wanted no extra advertising if I were to fail. When the play proved to be a success, I had someone else remove the stickers. As I look back, I think that I played one or two scenes rather well—better than I could play them now—just as by some happy accident, at fifteen

I did some drawings better than I could ever do them again. Though I was quite unused to serious values, there was in this performance in Justice something vital that came wholly from the desire to make good. Even though not backed up by the right technique, it had a certain gauche sincerity.

Justice, which had been produced in the late winter, ran till the middle of July, and the following fall I went out on the road, where it proved no great lure in many of the middle western cities. This play, which was responsible for certain reforms in British criminal jurisprudence, seemed very remote in many towns and cities where we were booked. In one place, I think it was Grand Rapids, I was informed by the press agents that they had arranged a marvelous stunt for me to do which would cause a healthy glow in the box office. I was to go to the leading department store and there autograph copies of Justice for anyone who brought them in or would buy a copy in the book department. They broke this to me gradually. There was more to come. So that nothing of all this might be lost, I was to stand while inscribing the play books, behind a plate glass window, which, of course, they assured me would be tastefully decorated in a most literary and dignified way.

"Don't you think it's a good hunch?" they asked. "It'll be wonderful advertising."

I suggested to them that it would also be good advertising if I, like Lady Godiva, and in the same costume, were to ride through the town on the back of an elephant painted blue, holding in one hand the scales of Justice and in the other a placard with the name and location of the theater. In spite of the unleashed imagination of the press agents, and they actually performed, unaided by me, some of the dubious stunts they thought up, comparatively few people on the road were attracted by or seemed to want Justice.

I returned to New York in mid-season, confronted with the problem of what to do next. God help anyone after his first success in the theater! There is always the fear and the dread that it may be different next time. If one yields to the temptation to do again what he has succeeded in, there is the certainty that sooner or later his equipment will become exhausted. Some actors never exhaust their equipment till they are dead. Irving never did, but then, there are few Irvings.

Among other things that I considered to do next was the dramatization of DuMaurier's Peter Ibbetson. Of this book I had always had and still have the fondest recollections. Nothing pleased me more mightily than when in London last winter, Gerald DuMaurier gave me an original drawing by his father and a notebook which had been used during the writing of Peter Ibbetson. On the last page of this is the family tree of the Ibbetsons, showing the lineage of

Feb 19th 1925

Dear Jack

I send you this sketch of my father on the first night of your Hamlet in London in deep friendship

Gerald du Maurier

A leaf from Du Maurier's note book presented to the author by the artist's son, Gerald Du Maurier, the actor, on Barrymore's opening night of *Hamlet* in London

© *Courtesy Messrs. Shubert, producers of the play*

John Barrymore as Peter Ibbetson

Peter, with his delightful French ancestry. It is a charming thing to possess, being so typical of the gayety and beauty of the author's mind.

I had often talked with Constance Collier about doing Ibbetson together; she owned the dramatic rights, but nothing ever came of our talks. We were both free at this time, and there was a prospect that we could get my brother Lionel to play Colonel Ibbetson. The only difficulty was to get a management and a theater. I went to see Al Woods, who had been my manager both in a play I like to forget, called The Yellow Ticket, and in Kick-in. "Al," I said, "I've got a play, but I don't want you to read it."

"I suppose you just want me to give you the theater and pay the bills."

"Yes, that's about what I want."

"What's the play like?"

"Oh, you wouldn't like it; it's full of dreams. It's called Peter Ibbetson, by a guy named Du-

Maurier. I'm going to play Peter, Constance Collier is going to be the Duchess of Towers and Lionel is coming back from the movies to the theater, and he's going to play Colonel Ibbetson, my uncle."

"That's pretty good; can't you tell me anything about it at all?"

"Well, there's one scene in it where Lionel calls me a bastard and I hit him over the head with a club and knock him cold. It's the end of the second act."

"You're on, kid. I'll take it."

Al Woods is, to my mind, one of the most interesting figures in the theatrical world. He pretends not to know about things, whereas his grasp of the details and business side of theatrical management is extremely comprehensive. It was not mere luck that turned the impresario of such significant sensations as Nellie, The Beautiful Cloak Model, into one of the leading producers of Forty-second Street.

We went at the production of Peter Ibbetson with the greatest delight. We were all so fond of the book and had been for so long that we wanted to get everything in that would please the people who knew the story. We even went so far as to figure out what the loathsome scent would be that Colonel Ibbetson used. Before the scene where I killed him, Lionel took great pains to douse himself with this so that I should get a strong whiff of it when I was near him. My adoration of the drawings was so great that I made myself up to look exactly like them and wore a beard. The late Sir Herbert Beerbohm Tree, when he came to the theater one night in New York, was very charming about the performance and the production, but referring to my beard, he said: "That fellow looks so like a dentist. If you don't shave him instantly, the romance will fly out of the window."

These things which we did in our excessive zeal to preserve the book meant nothing to the spectators; but a certain inherent beauty, an arresting nostalgia of the story did get into the dramatization and kept audiences spellbound and quiet, even during the terrible first night in New York when the properties acted up and in the dream scenes the scenery fell over, disclosing shirt-sleeved stage hands, guy ropes and brick walls. On the second night most of this happened again and the company was unable to give on either occasion a real performance. But through it all the play obtained, and at subsequent performances became a great success.

I know of no play with which I have ever been connected at which audiences were so largely made up of people who had already seen the play. At every performance there were repeaters. One woman in New York told me that she had seen Peter Ibbetson forty-five times. It was war time, and the scenes in which the past was lived again and there were reunions with loved ones were very comforting to many persons. When we played it in Canada, where so many people had lost sons, the sympathy for the play was most unusual. This quiet, peculiar appeal hardly seemed like the theater.

After Peter Ibbetson, I had my choice of two plays. One of them was Barrie's Dear Brutus. The leading part of this was sympathetic and good, and when I read the play it seemed difficult to see how anybody could fail, even if he were only able to give one-tenth as good a performance as was given by Gerald Du-Maurier in London. I knew that the play could not help succeeding in New York, and worse than that, if one played it in New York there would almost inevitably be a long road engagement. The least to be expected from Dear Brutus was two seasons.

So I elected to do the other play which was offered to me, an English version of Tolstoy's play, The Living Corpse, which we called Redemption. My wife made the adaptation, but it wasn't credited to her on the play bills. She had from the first been enthusiastic to have me do Redemption, and while I was hesitating about accepting Dear Brutus, she went to the sister of Joe Davidson, the sculptor, who was then running The Russian Inn in New York, and from her she obtained a literal translation. Out of this she made an excellent adaptation, which, like most good adaptations for the theater, contained a great deal that was original. I am certain that it was in a large measure responsible for the success of Redemption, a success which bewildered a great many people. At first the play did not do good business, because it was put on in the midst of the flu epidemic. As soon as this scare was over, however, and people began to go to the theater again, it became an established success.

I have never felt that my playing of it was particularly able, and there were portions of it that I never found very clear and consequently could not make them clear to audiences. In the first act, when I should have been a human being, I was given so many jewels and appurtenances to wear that I always seemed to myself a sweet-scented jackass. Till the last act, where there was great reality, I was never on the balls of my feet. Occasionally, I think I was good in that last act. As everyone knows, Redemption is one of those gloomy depictions of a Russian soul in especial agony, and only rarely is there a mild bit of cheer or color.

One night my brother came to see the play, and near him was a girl who munched chocolates diligently all through the performance. When in desperation at the futility of life I stood before a mirror to shoot myself, she said in a loud, nasal voice to her companion: "Oh, the poor pru-in." I fear that in that line the voice of many persons spoke, though perhaps they would not agree with the pronunciation.

One night, in changing a scene, the mirror

before which I stood when I was about to shoot myself was broken and there was no time to get another. So that I might be looking at something before I pulled the trigger, the frame was left on the wall and asphaltum, which is ever ready in the theater to touch up scenery, was daubed in the frame where the glass should have been. After that performance, a friend of mine who is a painter came back to my dressing room and after telling me some nice things about my performance, said: "What a perfectly wonderful touch that was of Tolstoy's—that a man about to kill himself should, before doing so, go look at a painting of a landscape." The artist in him spoke. Each to his trade.

Before we did Peter Ibbetson I had purchased the rights to do Sem Benelli's play, La Cena delle Beffe which was called in English The Jest. Both Ned Sheldon, who made the English version, and I thought that this would be a very good play for Lionel and myself to do

© *Photo by Alfred Cheney Johnston*

Lionel Barrymore in *The Jest*

Photo by Charlotte Fairchild

Lionel Barrymore in the Third Act of *The Copperhead*

together. There was a great part in it for him, and it seemed almost criminal that he should not be back in the theater to play it. He was doing extremely well in the movies, not only acting, but also at odd moments and in various bars, suggesting with extraordinary imagination, a great many of the most distinguished producers' two-reelers. Most of his ideas were received with mild amusement, but later they almost invariably had an odd way of appearing on the screen. Though we owned The Jest before Peter Ibbetson was produced, the conditions were not right for its production, and consequently Lionel's return to the stage was as Colonel Ibbetson, in which his success was tremendous.

Before we produced The Jest, Lionel had made a great hit in The Copperhead. The old man in the last acts of this was as different from the part he played in The Jest as any two parts in the theater could possibly be, and yet no critic mentioned this extraordinary versatility. We thought The Jest would be an artistic success that would run about six weeks, make little or no money, and then go to the storehouse. We felt that the play was a sound one and very good theater, and as it had so much of the Renaissance we thought that it would be great fun to put it on.

Predicting the length of a run is always hazardous. We were quite wrong. In production The Jest proved gory, passionate, colorful and provocative. Audiences did not seem to mind that the play was not exactly a moral one. They didn't care that it was like a bullfight in a brothel, punctuated by occasional flashes of lightness. They did not seem to be able to get enough of The Jest and it ran and ran.

After the fun of solving the difficulties was over and the play settled down to sure success, I became very tired of the patchoulied neurasthenic that I was called upon to play. This character has been variously described. One of the critics referred to it as a pallid but "mordauntly beautiful" young sensualist. With the blond wig and the very long green tights, it seems to me now that pictorically I must have appeared like a stained glass window of a decadent string bean. When we took The Jest off for the production of Richard III, the houses were still packed.

The first thought of my playing Richard III came about in an odd way. I was at the Bronx Zoo one day with Ned Sheldon looking at a red tarantula which had a gray bald spot on its back. This had been caused by trying to get out of its cage. It was peculiarly sinister and evil looking; the personification of a crawling power. I said to Sheldon: "It looks just like Richard III."

"Why don't you play it?" was his only comment.

Many of my friends had wanted me to do

Hamlet first. Now I may not have been wise to do Hamlet when I did, but I am certain it was wiser to act Richard first. Going into this was quite a stunt and involved a good deal of hard work; but I never like to talk about hard work, for no one believes it anyway, nor does the average outsider or layman consider that creative work is especially difficult. I had to make over my voice and work unceasingly on intonations. I am afraid that when I came to the playing, I probably, with no intention of so doing, sang a great deal of the text.

Richard III was the definite result of months of labor; it was a meticulous and not particularly inspired performance. Occasionally, however, it was effective and great fun to do. The production by Robert Edmund Jones and Arthur Hopkins was extremely beautiful and much liked, I am sure. People have told me that they can recall few scenes in the theater that were so hauntingly beautiful as that of Richard on a

John Barrymore as Richard III

John Barrymore in *Clair de Lune*

white horse talking to the young princes before the tower. I could play the whole play a great deal better now, I am certain, but never again would I undertake to play it eight times a week.

After Richard III and before I played Hamlet in New York, Ethel and I appeared in Clair de Lune, which was written by my wife. This was a case of a play maimed by loving kindness, in which the author was slightly bewildered, but quite helpless. The only thing that I can think of that would correspond to what we did to this play would be, if when a débutante is going to her first party, instead of giving her a simple dress, in which her charm would be apparent, the family in their glutinous affection should deck her in everything but the kitchen stove. I know of nothing more that could have been done to distract attention from this charming play, except to have called upon Lionel to play a part in it. As it was, it seemed entirely filled with dwarfs and Barrymores.

And Clair du Lune should never have had all these trappings or have been made a vehicle for stars or box-office reputations.

Then came Hamlet. For several seasons people had been telling me that Hamlet was the logical play for me to do next, but I had never read it with the idea of acting it. Naturally, before I could make up my mind I wanted to go over the part carefully. I wanted to read and re-read it until I could find out what I could do with it or what it would do to me. I went down to White Sulphur Springs and went over the play for weeks. It was practically my first reading. Then I went out into the woods and rehearsed myself in parts of it. I was amazed to find how simple Hamlet seemed to be, and I was no little bewildered that anything of such infinite beauty and simplicity should have acquired centuries of comment. It seems to me that all the explanation, all the comment that is necessary upon Hamlet Goethe wrote in Wilhelm Meister. These simple words in short sentences, with which the editor of the Temple edition has had the wit to preface the text, are more illuminating than all the commentaries:

"And to me it is clear that Shakespere sought to depict a great deed laid upon a soul unequal to the performance of it. In this view I find the piece composed throughout. Here is an oak tree planted in a costly vase, which should have received into its bosom only lovely flowers; the roots spread out, the vase is shivered to pieces."

Hamlet to me in the theater. no matter who plays it, will never be quite the play that it is in the theater of the cerebellum. When one thinks how few illustrators add anything to a book—Howard Pyle added a great deal, but he was one of the few—it is not strange that the acting does not always add to or enhance the reading of Shakespere. Perhaps one of the reasons so many people write about Hamlet and do not write about other simple things of great beauty, like the Sermon on the Mount and the Gettysburg Speech, is merely because they feel they can add something to the character which no one else has done. They see themselves playing the part. I don't know whether it was Noah or P. T. Barnum who first said: "In every man there is a little of Hamlet." Seriously, I have often wondered why women go to see Hamlet in the theater. Perhaps it is because they bear male children. I don't know.

V

THE Theatre Royal, Haymarket, London, has a stage cat which is a privileged character. It is a huge tom-cat with a big, broad head. Just how long it has been in the theater, no one seems to know, nor what its life is outside of theater hours. In appearance it seems to be a bland combination of a conservative and a bum. I was told that during actual performances it was always locked up, but that during the preparation of a play it was accustomed to keep track of what was going on. At every one of our rehearsals of Hamlet, it was on the stage. It had a way of crossing back and forth with its tail in the air and sniffing slightly. It always did so during my soliloquies, and it was very disturbing. Nor did I quite like the way it looked at me. It seemed to say: "I've seen them all—what are you doing here?"

Don Marquis' famous cat, Mehitabel, in her wanderings in Greenwich Village last winter met an old theater cat that had played in the support of Forrest, Barrett, Booth and many others. This old-timer deplored bitterly the inadequacy of the race of present-day theater cats and touching his breast with a paw, said: "It's because they haven't got it here." The cat at The Haymarket was, I am sure, very like the cat Mehitabel met.

Herbert Waring, who played Polonius in the production of Hamlet, told a story about this Haymarket Theatre cat at a dinner which was given for me by the O. P. Club of London, an old organization which once a year gives a dinner to some stranger. A number of the company were also present, and they were called upon for speeches. After Israel Zangwill, who presided, Fay Compton, who was the Ophelia, Constance

Collier, who was the queen, myself and others had spoken, there was very little that was left to be said. The possibilities of the delightful occasion were vitiated, sucked and squeezed dry. Everything that could be told about the production had been used and much had been made of the entente cordiale. Still there was another speaker—Herbert Waring. I could see that he was apprehensive about what he was going to say, for bit by bit that he had thought of and had hoped to use himself was being said by others. When he rose he told this story about the Haymarket cat:

"Mr. Barrymore," he said, "had been sitting hunched up in the orchestra watching the last dress rehearsal. At the end he came upon the stage and complimented the members of the company in turn upon their work. He turned to Miss Compton and said: 'Miss Compton, yours will be the most enchanting and most adorable Ophelia since that of Ellen Terry. You combine virginal charm and wistfulness to a degree which I am sure has never been approximated. God bless you and thank you very much.' And then to Constance Collier: 'My dear Constance, I can't tell you how magnificent you are. You have invested this character with sensuous beauty, enhanced by a certain full-blown provocativeness which I feel certain is exactly what Shakspere meant. God bless you and thank you very much.'

" 'Mr. Keene,' he said, 'the King has usually been considered a bad part. I never thought so. Seeing you rehearse it to-night, I'm certain it isn't. God bless you and thank you very much.' Next came my turn. 'Mr. Waring, you will make a triumph that will be unprecedented as Polonius. Never before has the part been played with such a happy combination of glutinous sententiousness and senile verbosity, patined by a kindly wisdom. It is unique. God bless you and thank you very much.' 'Mr. Thorpe, the

© Courtesy of Famous Players

John Barrymore in *Dr. Jekyll and Mr. Hyde*

© Courtesy of Famous Players

ghost of Hamlet's father, I feel quite certain, has never been played as you play it. It is an onomatopoetic *tour de force*. With the assistance of the electrical equipment, you will be unforgettable and terrifying. God bless you and thank you very much.'

" 'Mr. Field, the first grave digger, has been played with everything from a red patch on the seat of the breeches to barnyard imitations to enhance the text. Without any of these accessories and with judicious cuts, you are extremely funny. It is a great gift. God bless you and thank you very much.' 'Horatio, all I can say about you is that you are like the Rock of Gibraltar, sprayed upon by the milk of human kindness. I feel than I can lean upon you. I shall probably have to. God bless you and thank you very much.' 'Laertes, you were a flaming ball of fire to-night, melting into tenderness at the proper moment. It was an excellent performance, particularly in the duel scenes where, without any apparent effort at self-protection, you seem always to be in the right place. God knows how you do it. God bless you and thank you very much.' 'Rosencrantz and Guildenstern, I imagine you know that for centuries these parts have been known as the sleeve links of the drama. Until to-night I have never been able to tell you apart, but you invest them with separate personalities. It is incredible. God bless you and thank you very much.'

"Even Hamlet's vocabulary, and by now he was an extremely tired Hamlet, was considerably exhausted. Just then the theater cat came on to the stage to see what it was all about, and Mr. Barrymore stooped over and stroked the large, square head: 'As for you, my dear fellow, you are going to make a hell of a hit in one of my soliloquies.' "

Hamlet was not put on in London until I had been through two years of the greatest disappointment. I had a very good company lined up, but I could not get a theater. Everyone I went to see was most cordial and kind, but no one had faith enough to help me. I could not altogether blame the lessees and managers of the London theaters, because Shakspere has not been particularly successful in the recent years in the West End. The plays of Shakspere are constantly and very beautifully played at The Old Vic, which, as I remember, is more North than West.

I'm not very good at talking business anyway, and I was very glad when in the various managerial offices the conversation could be changed from theater renting to fishing. I was always embarrassed at being turned down, but I became slightly hardened to it. I persisted because I was encouraged by the flattering success that I had had here as Hamlet. Arthur Hopkins, who was associated with me in the production in America, did not feel that there was anything but loss to be encountered with

Hamlet in London; and so he withdrew. But he was gracious enough to loan me the head electrician, the head carpenter and the stage manager of the American production. Without this trio, I should have been almost helpless.

Finally, after two years of negotiations that came to nothing, I met Frederick Harrison, who owns the Haymarket Theatre. He agreed to let me rent the house for six weeks. Half of the money for the production was raised in London; the other half I put up myself. Had it not been successful, I stood to lose twenty-five thousand dollars. No one could have been more gracious or more interested than Mr. Harrison was. At the end of the six weeks he postponed his own production of a new A. A. Milne play in order that Hamlet might run three weeks more.

I was particularly delighted to have the Haymarket Theatre, not only because it is the best in London, with a delightful staff and clientele, but because in this theater my father

John Barrymore as Hamlet

played many years ago. I never went into the stage door without smiling over a story that I had heard so often. The stage entrance is in a *cul-de-sac* street, and there is only one way in. One night my father and Charles Brookfield, who was, a few years ago, the play censor in England, were leaving the theater together. My father espied two bailiffs approaching and anticipated that they were for him, as they were. There being no other way out of the street, my father grabbed hold of the more athletic appearing of the two, and then shouted to Brookfield: "Run, Barry, run." There was nothing for Brookfield to do but to oblige by running, and when he had been given sufficient time for a get-away, my father, as Brookfield, apologized good-naturedly to the bailiff that he had detained. The other one made a feeble effort to follow Brookfield, who jumped into a cab and disappeared.

The rehearsals of Hamlet were more fun

than anything I ever have done. I had wanted to put it on in London so much, and one crashing disappointment after another merely made me keener to do so. There was another pleasure for me, and that was because I was doing the whole thing myself. In London I had no producer or director. This added responsibility was really a delight, as there was such a splendid sense of collaboration and helpfulness everywhere. The company was interested extraordinarily by the way in which the production was staged; this was quite new for Shakspere in London.

There was always a feeling of good humor and good fellowship on tap. I was explaining one day to the girls who carry on the body of Ophelia in the burial scene that, owing to the extraordinary and suggestive lighting of Robert E. Jones, they would not be recognized as having appeared in earlier scenes. I cautioned them that they should remember that in this scene they were virgins. One of them said to me:

"My dear Mr. Barrymore, we are not character actresses, we are extra ladies." This is the spirit in which the whole production was done.

Finally, the first night. The man in front of the house, who was diplomatic, courteous and dressed in evening clothes, as the business people of the English theaters always are, came back to me several times to tell me about the audience. He was full of the cause and his enthusiasm was so whole-hearted. "Of course, you know," he said, "Mr. Shaw is in the house." Next he came back to tell me: "With the greatest difficulty we just found two seats for Mr. Masefield." The effect of this upon a fairly nervous American in London, who is about to appear in the best play that England has produced, can well be imagined. But the man from the front of the house kept on—only mere time stopped him. He told me of the arrival of Dunsany, Maugham, Mary Anderson, that beloved actress of Shaksperean rôles, the Asquiths, Sir Anthony

Hope Hawkins, Henry Arthur Jones, Pontius Pilate, Paul of Tarsus and the Pope. Somehow, it did not add to my scare, for one had the same sense of detachment, I imagine, that one would feel on the route to the guillotine. I looked from the wreath that Madame Melba had sent me—the first I ever received—to the mounted tarpon caught off Key West, Florida, which had been inadvertently packed and sent to London by my colored valet. Fishing, I thought, will be just as good as ever when this is over.

I powdered the beads of sweat off the forehead and sauntered on to the stage smoking a cigarette. I wanted to put up a bluff of casualness to the other members of the company. It was much worse for me, playing Hamlet under my own management and direction in a new country, but I understood that they were apprehensive and I appreciated their reason for being so. There had only been time for one full dress rehearsal with the scenery, and it was complicated for persons not accustomed to it. Many of the entrances and exits were made by the steps that lead up to the massive arch which formed the permanent background of the entire production. I did the best I could to encourage them. I think this is the best performance I have ever given. No other make-believe that I have accomplished has been so authentic, I am sure, as my simulated calmness that night. Then came my own first scene. I threw my cigarette away and on the darkened stage I sat waiting for the curtain to go up. Those seconds that I sat there are reasonably unforgettable.

It was awfully pleasant to be in London, and just because I was playing something at a theater to be let in on so many things. It was charming to meet again the friends I had made in my school days. I went to see Ben Webster and Mrs. Webster, who had been so kind to me twenty years before when I used to go to their flat in Bedford Street from my school in Wimbledon. I saw the same old sofa where I slept when I could stay away from school. There were the identical books and pictures, and the whole place had managed to keep from change, as English flats are apt to do. Nor did the Websters look any older. And now their daughter was playing a small part in Hamlet.

It was a great pleasure, too, to renew my old friendship with Gerald DuMaurier. One day he told me that Sir Squire Bancroft, the dean of the English speaking stage, wished to see me. I went to his apartment in the Albany, where he has lived for years. He told me about Hamlets that he had seen and suggested many things which I might do in the part. His ideas were so illuminating and so amazingly modern. He was so helpful and interested. "Did you ever hear of this bit of business?" he would ask, and then he would illustrate what he meant. He came one day with some grandnieces to a mat-

The author with a day's catch off Cornwall

John Barrymore—a drawing by John Singer Sargent

inée and sat in the box of the theater that he had once owned. He suggested that I use a device that Fechter had employed effectively. I did not adopt this particular suggestion because it was out of line with what I felt I could do, but since he had been so gracious and helpful, I suddenly decided, when I saw him sitting there that afternoon, to incorporate the idea. It was at the end of the soliloquy in the first act and the other members of the company were crowding in the wings waiting for the call at the end of the act. They could not, because of the nature of the scenery, see what was going on on the stage and when the curtain did not come down as ordinarily, they thought that Hamlet had really gone mad.

I saw Sir Squire Bancroft again the night the Garrick Club gave a dinner for me. We assembled in an upper room, and then this distinguished, white-haired man escorted me down the broad circular steps to the room where the dinner was to be held. On the way we passed one after another of those eighteenth and early nineteenth century portraits of great actors and actresses of the English stage. Suddenly I remembered my grandmother, and I could understand their apparent look of whimsical austerity. An American Hamlet in London!

A supper in a loft over a tavern was given for me one night by an organization known as The Gallery First-nighters. They had all been to Hamlet. They had expected a speech and they asked a number of questions, but it didn't go very well and I was grateful when the chairman suggested that like the Jongleur de Notre Dame, who had no gift but his juggling, the actor's business was to act. They therefore called upon me for something from Hamlet. Though the party was informal, I had another engagement afterwards and was dressed. I told them: "It isn't easy to indulge in Danish ruminations when one is dressed like a waiter." As soon as my soliloquy was over, it was a very amusing evening, for these first-nighters of the gallery were genuinely interested in the theater.

I was saddened during my London engagement by the death of John Sargent. In Whistler's old house I had lived next to him in Tite Street during the first year I was trying to put on Hamlet in London. Only two winters ago when I was playing Hamlet in Boston, Sargent made a sketch of me. My wife was very anxious that I have this done. He told me that his portrait-painting days were over, but that he would make a sketch. I was to pay him a thousand dollars. When he had finished it, he wrote upon it: "To my friend, John Barrymore," and refused to take any money, though it had been a commission. He said: "It's a Christmas present for you."

At the end of the engagement of nine weeks, Hamlet closed. The run could not be extended because some of the cast were under contract to appear in other plays. The last night I look back to as the pleasantest I have ever spent in the theater. There was enthusiasm all through the play, and at the end, when I stood with the company to acknowledge the applause, there were cries of "Come back." After the play I gave a party on the stage of the theater for the entire company, the stage hands, the carpenters, the electricians, and everyone connected with the Haymarket Theatre in any capacity whatsoever. The charwomen and cleaners sat upon the steps of Elsinore and drank Cointreau, thinking, I'm afraid, that it wasn't very good gin.

There is always someone who, when you have been regarding a charming this, calls your attention to a not so entrancing that. A few days after Hamlet was produced in London, I received the following letter from G. Bernard Shaw:

"22nd February, 1925.

"My dear Mr. Barrymore: I have to thank you for inviting me—and in such kind terms too—to your first performance of Hamlet in London; and I am glad you had no reason to complain of your reception, or, on the whole, of your press. Everyone felt that the occasion was one of extraordinary interest; and so far as your personality was concerned they were not disappointed.

"I doubt, however, whether you have been able to follow the course of Shakespearean production in England during the last fifteen years or so enough to realize the audacity of your handling of the play. When I last saw it performed at Stratford-on-Avon, practically the entire play was given in three hours and three quarters, with one interval of ten minutes; and it made the time pass without the least tedium, though the cast was not in any way remarkable. On Thursday last you played five minutes longer with the play cut to ribbons, even to the breath-bereaving extremity of cutting out the recorders, which is rather like playing King John without little Arthur.

"You saved, say, an hour and a half on Shakespear by the cutting, and filled it up with an interpolated drama of your own in dumb show. This was a pretty daring thing to do. In modern shop plays, without characters or anything but the commonest dialogue, the actor has to supply everything but the mere story, getting in the psychology between the lines, and presenting in his own person the fascinating hero whom the author has been unable to create. He is not substituting something of his own for something of the author's: he is filling up a void and doing the author's work for him. And the author ought to be extremely obliged to him.

"But to try this method on Shakespear is to take on an appalling responsibility and put up a staggering pretension. Shakespear, with all his

The author in a characteristic pose

Photo by Melbourne Spurr

The most recent portrait of the author

shortcomings, was a very great playwright; and the actor who undertakes to improve his plays undertakes thereby to excel to an extraordinary degree in two professions in both of which the highest success is extremely rare. Shakespear himself, though by no means a modest man, did not pretend to be able to play Hamlet as well as write it; he was content to do a recitation in the dark as the ghost. But you have ventured not only to act Hamlet, but to discard about a third of Shakespear's script and substitute stuff of your own, and that, too, without the help of dialogue. Instead of giving what is called a reading of Hamlet, you say, in effect, 'I am not going to read Hamlet at all: I am going to leave it out. But see what I give you in exchange!'

"Such an enterprise must justify itself by its effect on the public. You discard the recorders as hackneyed back chat, and the scene with the king after the death of Polonius, with such speeches as 'How all occasions do inform against me!' as obsolete junk, and offer instead a demonstration of that very modern discovery called the Œdipus complex, thereby adding a really incestuous motive on Hamlet's part to the merely conventional incest of a marriage (now legal in England) with a deceased husband's brother. You change Hamlet and Ophelia into Romeo and Juliet. As producer, you allow Laertes and Ophelia to hug each other as lovers instead of lecturing and squabbling like hectoring big brother and little sister: another complex!

"Now your success in this must depend on whether the play invented by Barrymore on the Shakespear foundation is as gripping as the Shakespear play, and whether your dumb show can hold an audience as a straightforward reading of Shakespear's rhetoric can. I await the decision with interest.

"My own opinion is, of course, that of an author. I write plays that play for three hours and a half even with instantaneous changes and only one short interval. There is no time for silences or pauses: the actor must play on the line and not between the lines, and must do nine-tenths of his acting with his voice. Hamlet—Shakespear's Hamlet—can be done from end to end in four hours in that way; and it never flags nor bores. Done in any other way Shakespear is the worst of bores, because he has to be chopped into a mere cold stew. I prefer my way. I wish you would try it, and concentrate on acting rather than on authorship, at which, believe me, Shakespear can write your head off. But that may be vicarious professional jealousy on my part.

"I did not dare to say all this to Mrs. Barrymore on the night. It was chilly enough for her without a coat in the stalls without any cold water from

"Yours perhaps too candidly,

"G. Bernard Shaw."

Not as a result of this letter, but because I like to interlard work in the theater with the making of movies, which I thoroughly enjoy, I am back in Hollywood once more working upon a new picture. It is made from a great classic of American literature, Melville's Moby Dick. This book appeals to me and always has. It has an especial appeal now, for in the last few years, both on the stage and on the screen, I have played so many scented, bepuffed, bewigged and ringletted characters—princes and kings, and the like—that I revel in the rough and almost demoniacal character, such as Captain Ahab becomes in the last half of the picture after his leg has been amputated by Moby Dick, the white whale. What we are going to do for a love interest, I don't quite know. He might fall in love with the whale. I am sure, however, Hollywood will find a way.

THE END